# THE DISAPPEARING MERCHANT

MIKE HOGENMILLER

ISBN: 978-0-578-54397-0

Printed in the United States of America

# PROLOGUE

THE WORLD IS CHANGING.

It's interesting to watch the changes taking place and it's entirely possible most people won't even recognize or notice most of them. Each morning, it seems we wake up to a completely different environment than the one we experienced the previous day. A prime example? The 2016 Presidential Election, no matter which way you voted. With both positive and negative results, these evolutions impact us on a social, economic, and environmental level. This book is dedicated to the changes that have taken place over the last 25 years of a rewarding 40-year career in retail. To be more precise, it revolves around my experience in procurement, buying, merchandising, and product acquisition...whatever you'd like to call it. But in the end, the abilities I developed defined my specific role as a ***merchant***. These important, specialized skills are now most likely disappearing from the current buying environment.

I retired from the retail industry in 2016. In what felt like an instant, several suppliers approached me for help in developing strategies for dealing with the buying community. They asked me to engage in a variety of business situations in the retail industry for the benefit of the supplier. Most of the work I take on is a direct result of the interactions between a buyer and a supplier which are, without intention, driving negative results for one or both in the relationship. In my post-retirement role, I've come to a personal realization that while there is an improvement in the quality of the decisions being made by buyers, there is also a significant decline in their abilities to build meaningful relationships with suppliers -- the hallmark of a good merchant. Often, it can be attributed to merchants evolving into what some in the industry have called "cost focused buyers," "data scientists," or a combination of the two. In many cases, the consequences of the shift from merchant to cost buyer or data scientist substantially diminishes the value of the relationships between suppliers and buyers.

I have always agreed that the availability of improved technology has driven new, accessible, real-time data and accelerated the speed with which decisions can be made. This added information has also optimized accuracy, provided more detailed opportunities, and improved the customer experience in general. However, I take issue with the talent we have lost and continue to lose as a by-product of this change. It has led to a significant gap in merchant development, which could result in losing this particular type of talent altogether in the future. In fact, such an outcome is inevitable if we continue to focus solely on data to support speed and accuracy and fail to factor relationship-building abilities into the equation. The last 25 years of my career were the most meaningful. The lessons I learned were vital, especially for the benefit of the consumer, who could be getting lost in the shuffle and losing some of the opportunistic value as a result.

This book represents an opportunity for the industry to address the loss of talent that results from being a cost buyer, a data scientist, or any combination of the two, instead of a true merchant. Its intent is to:

- Influence the industry to think about mutual objectives with suppliers and well-defined mutual accountability.
- Mitigate the perceived risk in the relationship, whether real or fabricated, that drives up costs and creates a negative impact as a result.
- Realize mutually beneficial results between retailers and suppliers that ultimately lead to a higher level of overall value for the consumer.

# 1

# SO, WHAT'S THE BIG DEAL?

THE BIG DEAL is that the behavioral mannerisms in which products and services are procured can impact the final cost/value proposition to the consumer or end user. Since the beginning of time, merchants have traveled the world looking for opportunities to buy and sell whatever underdeveloped trade they could support. Their success depended upon their ability to understand the communities they served, and as a result, what products were necessary for the survival or improvement of the consumers' environment. It was also important to develop and maintain a relationship based on trust with their suppliers. Today it's no different, but there's one critical exception: we have built a significant cost over time around risk because of deteriorating relationships between buyers and suppliers.

Think about your own finances and what you may or may not do to mitigate risk. Most may need a savings reserve to respond to unforeseen emergencies which could include the loss of an income source, car and home repairs, or medical bills. Imagine if you could use that funding, or at least a sizable portion of it, to invest in your future or improve your family's quality of life. All you need is a significant reduction in the likelihood of these unwanted outcomes. It signifies the difference in how a consumer manages their own personal affairs and relationships, and how much risk they are willing to absorb as a result.

It's the same principle with respect to the acquisition of products or services. Many of the risks, real or unreal, are caused by a buyer -- the direct result of how they manage supplier relationships. It's quite possible much of that risk and the cost associated with it can be mitigated and returned to the consumer simply by changing behaviors. It starts with the initial conversation between the buyer and the supplier and their subsequent relationship, which most often is driven by the attitudes and behaviors of the buyer. The goal? Be a true merchant who provides maximum value to the consumer, while reducing risk for both the supplier and the organization they work for. Remember, the associated risk and cost created by the buyer is incurred primarily by the supplier and passed along to the consumer in the form of higher prices. To reach authentic merchant status, the buyer must manage the defined costs and the relationship by removing risk. Buyers must also stop committing the common behavioral sins in which one spends time and cost creating risk throughout the relationship. The cost of risk and the percentage it represents in the overall cost of the product or service could be significant depending on the amount of ambiguity in the relationship between a buyer and a supplier.

Think of a simple cost equation from a supplier like this: raw materials + manufacturing + G&A + supply chain and distribution + marketing + gross margin + risk = cost. All aspects of the cost equation are well-defined, except for risk, which could represent one of the highest contributors to cost, driving a significant loss of value. If you look more closely at the equation, you can estimate each cost (except for risk) with specifics derived from the available data. Risk is ever evolving and hardly ever controllable by a buyer without the appropriate behaviors.

- With all the data available for us to evaluate, the most important - risk - has no line-item value.
- This same view of cost can be equally applied to products or services because both are a direct result of the relationship and how it's structured between supplier and buyer.
- Risk is the direct result of a supplier building costs into the product associated with not knowing what the buyer is going to ask for or when.
- The less structure or trust in the relationship, the more built-in cost by the supplier.

# 2
# WHEN/WHY DID IT HAPPEN?

The original merchant had very little data on products or services bought or the reasons behind their cost. He or she depended upon their experience and trusted in their relationships with a variety of suppliers to ensure they bought items at the right cost and best quality to create an overall value to the consumer. In addition, the merchant relied heavily on the customer to provide vocalized feedback to validate and improve their competitive position in the market. Consider this: until the mid-to-late 1970s, there was minimal data regarding individual products sold; no barcodes or computer identifying numbers. Instead, everything had a paper ticketed price and store associates or supplier representatives (via count books, etc.) manually tracked sales. It was a data-deprived market. The result? Merchant/supplier relationships were built on trust - and many times, that trust provided the sole reason for a merchant to buy from a particular source and vice-versa. As a merchant, you had to meet and talk with your suppliers and customers face-to-face on a regular basis to develop structured relationships and stay ahead of the market. Being a merchant was primarily a skill and an art with little science to support it.

As individualized detailed data became increasingly available, merchants began to spend an inordinate amount of time pouring over it to identify cost opportunities being driven by the company's performance expectations. As more data was uncovered, more parameters driving performance improvement metrics surfaced. More importantly, companies became more dependent and laser-focused on data, which resulted in the inevitable -- very detailed and defined bonus and individualized salary structures based on data performance. We officially entered the stage of the possibility for "paralysis by analysis" and rapidly moved from a merchant-based structure primarily founded upon skill and art, to a cost-buying platform driven by data analytics at the expense of merchant/supplier relationships. "Data science, "as it has been termed, tipped the scales away from merchants to cost buyers and data scientists. It's a scenario where science became the driving factor and the need for skill or art whether intentional or not, was significantly diminished.

Prior to the age of data, merchants were focused on general sales and profitability to earn a living, a direct result of the limited information they had. Although data does drive several positive opportunities in the market today, it has shifted the focus of buyers to more detailed and forever evolving sets of data. This latest information is normally structured around improvements in a variety of metrics that could include:

- Turns
- GMROI
- Unit Sales
- Dollar Sales, etc.

Depending upon the focus of the day, there's also a newer

and wider variety of parameters that could entail but are not limited to:

- Space productivity
- Sales by Price Point
- Unit Transactions
- Customer Demographics
- Consumer Bounce Rates
- Conversion Rates
- Return Rates
- Sales by Defined Customer
- Sales by Defined Channel
- Cost of Delivery by Channel
- Percentage of Imports vs. Domestic Purchases

Each new data set drives a different range of behaviors for buyers and a new platform of challenges for the suppliers. Often there is little or no discussion between the two parties as to how or why these challenges came about or the desired end result. RISK is now a significant factor in the realized cost of goods and services on the supplier side of the equation. Unfortunately, it is not recognized by the industry buyers as one of the most controllable.

# 3

# THE 10 SINS OF A BUYER

The cost of risk can either be instantaneous or develop over time. Ultimately, it is a derivative of buyer behavior in how and when it occurs. In today's market, there are several examples of critical behaviors and how they incur risk/cost on a regular basis. It's important to understand why each behavior occurs and what the impact is as a result.

## Sin #1

## Not Taking a Call or Responding to the Communication from a Supplier Who Is New to the Organization or Industry

This type of behavior often results in the buyer developing a reputation for ignoring the market, failing to understand the full competitive landscape, and having a lack of knowledge of who and what is being sold in the market. Buyers who tend to ignore suppliers who are new to the organization or industry have lost many opportunities. It's an egotistical attitude to always assume you are buying at the lowest cost from the best supplier, resulting in the maximized value available in the market (more on cost vs. value later).

At a minimum, vetting the supplier and understanding their competitive position in the market and the products they sell must be an expectation -- not a "when or if we have time." In addition, cultivating an open relationship with the total supplier base could make the difference in being the first or the last to learn about critical changes unfolding in the market. The risk? Paying a higher cost, culminating in a lower value for the consumer due to a lack of knowledge on the total market's structure. This could also result in being last to market with new products which creates significant cost risk because of a possible loss of market share. It takes discipline and organizational skills to prevent these unwanted outcomes.

- **Prioritization** - A merchant prioritizes their workload to ensure there is time for open communication with the total supplier market. This behavior takes a significant skill, one that is recognized by merchants but not by buyers.
- **Person-to-Person Conversation** - Many companies mistakenly believe they have mitigated risk through their participation in annual buying fairs and/or online or virtual introductions accessible by potential suppliers, etc. Unfortunately, the failure to engage in person-to-person conversation on a regular basis will ultimately result in a significant loss of opportunities.
- **Real-Time Learning** - Instead of once a year or whenever they decide to check the web when someone reminds them to, the merchant takes a proactive approach to real-time learning as it occurs.

**Sin #2**

### Ignoring the Calls or Creating a Significant Delay in Responding to Communication from an Existing Supplier

Suppliers are managing multiple competing buyers in a complex matrix of who-gets-what-products-when, and at what cost. This matrix includes several inputs: volume, distribution methods, targeted end-user, and of course, risk driven by their individual buyer relationships. Imagine a supplier giving a directive to its sales team to go out and communicate a change in their products -- whether it be cost, packaging, discontinued items, new items, and so on. ***The competing buyer with the most developed and open relationship will most likely obtain this information first.*** It creates a competitive benefit in being first to market regarding any change. The result of not responding or delaying communication adds risk in terms of cost of lost sales or delay in obtaining the benefit of the change.

For example, if it is a new product, the first buyer to the market receives the largest benefit by being exclusive whether negotiated with the supplier or not, until the others catch up. A supplier is usually anxious to obtain the market benefit of launching new products...and those customers who get there first are going to receive the most benefit and attention. This also has a long-term benefit for the retail outlet because over time consumers and suppliers will recognize those businesses that are most often the first to market. If its lower cost being communicated, the first buyer to enact the change gets the largest benefit by either driving a higher margin sooner or lowering their cost and retails to create a competitive advantage, and so on and so on. A buyer's lack of organization results in poor planning and a lack of prioritization of actions. In many cases, buyers blame the suppliers for not recognizing a change in the market they most likely missed; merchants are quick to recognize and evaluate change in a timely manner because of a suppliers' communication. The result is a strategically developed buyer-supplier relationship which benefits all involved as changes in the market occur.

## Sin #3
## Ignoring the Important Short- and Long-Term Goals of a Supplier

As a merchandising executive with responsibilities for large merchant/supplier relationships, I made it a habit to ask the supplier a critical question: "What are the three key objectives you are working on regarding our business relationship over the next 12 months?"

On purpose, I never asked the question publicly or in front of the buyer who managed this supplier. What's interesting is that the answers I received were usually well thought-out and had specific results in mind. The supplier was extremely focused on these projects and the expected beneficial outcomes. When I posed the same question to the responsible buyer without the presence of the same supplier, the responses I received in many cases was a completely different set of objectives. With conflicting objectives between the supplier and the buyer, each one's ability to drive success and maximize their own results was significantly diminished, if not impossible. Often, they were working *against* each other. ***In a true partnership, a merchant listens intently to the goals of a supplier and aligns them with their own.*** To achieve mutually beneficial results, both parties in the merchant/supplier relationship must work toward them in a synergistic manner. It's equally important to establish short- and long-term agreed-upon goals with documented toll gates and shared accountability (more on this later).

### Sin #4
### Allowing the Organization to Run the Relationship Between the Supplier and the Buyer

This is probably the most chronic and costly activity a company can be engaged in. Over time, new business channels have surfaced, resulting in a much more complex organization - especially when they all reside under one roof. New methods of consumer purchases outside of the traditional brick-and-mortar channel can include:

- Buy in Store, Pick up in Store
- Buy in Store, Deliver to Home
- Buy Online, Deliver to Home
- Buy Online, Pick Up in Store
- Buy Online, Return in Store
- Same-Day Delivery
- Job Site Delivery, etc.

All have created new channels of data and associated cost opportunities. In many cases, what has occurred is various parts of the organization now have different goals driving different behaviors. For example, if the supply chain group is charged with reducing supply chain costs, their requests to a supplier could involve changing packaging, increasing or decreasing pack quantities, or a change in shipping origins, among others. All involve costs to the supplier that most likely have not been planned into the business and will ultimately be passed along somewhere in the relationship. If all the company's organizational groups representing divergent functions with their own goals have direct access to the supplier, the ensuing confusion and loss of control of the business can drive substantial increases in cost. Suppliers end up reducing costs in one area and just placing it in another, resulting in a shell game that is difficult to uncover. Equate this to multiple air traffic controllers simultaneously giving direction to a single aircraft: the result is a zig-zag path vs. a direct flight pattern. This scenario comes with significantly higher costs. If there is a single owner with responsibility for prioritizing objectives and defining end results, these costs are no longer hidden. If managed correctly, they can become joint opportunities and are appropriately planned into the business over time. It has become vitally important to define a single owner who is supported without disruption by organizational groups responsible for uncovering opportunities for improvement through their subject matter expertise.

A merchant:

- Takes Ownership of the Relationship
- Recognizes Opportunities Defined by the Organization
- Plans and Manages These Opportunities into the Short-Term or Long-Term Objectives within Each Supplier

A merchant does NOT engage in this activity at the expense of the supplier or allow the organization to drive the relationship because he or she knows that this behavior only creates confusion and increases risk.

### Sin #5
### Poor Planning and the Ensuing Unreasonable Expectations

When an organization uncovers unexpected cost issues, many times they place the burden on the suppliers. Why? Because they can.... they see themselves as the customer with the right to make demands. It's the path to resolution with the least resistance as all it requires is for them to communicate the issue, which they expect the supplier to cover by providing a reduced cost. Most often, they insinuate a loss of business if the supplier refuses to acquiesce to their demands. You could term this as the "*because I said so*" and "*do it, or else*" attitudes. This is probably the most destructive behavior an organization can exhibit; it's incredibly damaging to a relationship. For example, a company may experience a sudden rise in shrink which negatively impacts gross margins and ultimately, profitability. The company directive could be for the increased cost to be covered by the buyers through margin improvements. For the buyer, there are two paths: get a lower cost from the supplier or raise your retails. The latter is the least attractive to the buyer, due to the possibility of driving short-term risk by damaging sales through loss of competitiveness. However, the worst behavior a buyer can engage in is to ask the supplier to cover the cost with no expectations for recovery. Unfortunately, it's a very common occurrence to simply pass one's unexpected expenses along to someone else to mitigate -- and it's a terrible practice for either side of the equation. A merchant will certainly follow the company initiatives, but with a mutually agreed upon strategy with the supplier. He or she will weigh all the options available without pushing the total expense on the supplier. These could include in this example:

- Strategic price increases to the consumer that do not create a competitive advantage for others in the market to cover the additional cost, (keep in mind this doesn't solve the original problem)

- Full examination and analysis of the details to understand the specifics in terms of the origins of the additional loss.
- Working with the supplier to identify and support initiatives both agree on which solves for the unexpected increased cost through new efficiencies or changes in process.

When specific cause and effect details are identified, shrink for example becomes a joint effort between the supplier and the merchant to solve. If left uncontrolled, it inevitably means lost business for both. Therefore, as business partners, the merchant and the supplier must take equal responsibility for identifying and solving the challenges that arise, regardless of their nature or origin.

### Sin #6

### Surprising a Supplier with the Loss of Business

While it is unfortunate, situations arise where a business realizes the necessity to change a supplier or remove specific products from its assortment. There are many valid reasons for this that could include but are not limited to:

- An Uncompetitive Cost
- New Product available to the Market not Available from an Existing Source
- Irreversible Deterioration in Quality
- Poor Delivery Performance, etc.

Many of these outcomes can be caused by the lack of an open relationship between supplier and buyer. Due to poor planning, they are usually unforeseen. For example, if a merchant creates a poor product development or vitality plan with a supplier and doesn't set long-term goals for product improvements and new product development, they can find themselves in an upside-down position in the market as other competitors move forward.

Normally, these types of situations result from poorly designed relationships, with little- to- no understanding of the changing market. When a supplier loses a buyer's business, it should never be a surprise, regardless of the size of the loss. A merchant should engage their supplier in a discussion as to why their company is considering a change and give the supplier a reasonable opportunity to correct or address the situation. While a high fear factor surrounding the potential loss of business may feel like leverage to a buyer, in fact it is intimidation - which is detrimental to a company's reputation.

The result? The supplier builds a substantial amount of cost into the relationship due to the risk of losing business with minimal, if any, communication on the matter. A merchant will work with a supplier regarding challenging issues that could arise from either side to formulate a plan that includes identifying the root cause with a path to joint resolution on an agreed upon timeline. Could it still result in a change of suppliers? Yes, but in this case the supplier will walk away feeling like they have been treated fairly, and your organization maintains or improves its reputation. If the issue is resolved without a supplier change, the result will be continued improvement in the relationship, which will drive long-term value, trust, and reduced cost through mitigated risk.

## Sin #7

## Being Friends Instead of Business Partners

It's difficult to count the number of times in my career that "name-dropping" was a preferred method of doing business. Too many times buyers and company executives become "friends" with their suppliers. At some point, buyers will realize the friendship was based solely on the buyer's access to a "pen" that held an authorization to sign a purchase order for goods or services. Once the pen is gone, so is the friendship. While some relationships develop into true friendships over time, it's never good for business. In this case, the perceptions are more dangerous than reality. Friendships with suppliers drive costly behaviors for buyers that can include but are not limited to:

- Looking the other way at times regarding issues or problems that arise with a friend vs a supplier.
- Becoming distracted by the friendship, which allows the buyer to avoid imposing the same short- or long-term necessary demands on friends vs suppliers.
- Leaning towards decisions which benefit friends vs being good for business and fair to the total supplier base.
- Being put in compromising positions because of time spent away from the business with a friend that wouldn't occur with other suppliers, e.g. dinners, vacations, entertainment events, etc., regardless of who is paying the bill. It's not about honesty, it's about perception.

The end result? Suppliers in general know who the "friends" are, and which relationships impact their ability to do business. These considerations will be included in their own calculated risk factors. A merchant understands the appropriate line between being friends vs. being business partners. Dinners or meals in general are fine, if in fact, they occur during normal business practices such as trade shows, annual supplier meetings, etc. But when they are 100 percent social in nature and/or recurring, they must be discouraged and discontinued. Let the buyer beware: there are suppliers whose primary goal is to become "friends." Avoid this circumstance every time.

## Sin #8

## Buyer-Caused Ambiguity in the Relationship

Having a discussion or engaging in activity with little or no defined purpose can drive a dangerous wedge between the supplier community and a buyer. The cost from the supplier that goes along with the associated ambiguity can substantially increase over time. Buyers regularly engage in potential relationships with new suppliers, or with existing suppliers who are introducing their latest items, by testing product. If the test has no documented success parameters -- meaning both the supplier and the buyer don't understand or have not agreed on the intent and what result the buyer is working towards -- then this activity yields minimal, if any value, especially for the supplier.

In addition, after the completion of the exercise, if the test does not result in a defined action. e.g. the vendor is awarded the business should the test be successful and if so, how much and when, then the likelihood of the supplier making new product offers to the buyer in the future is substantially diminished. Buyers tend to engage in this type of activity on a regular basis because it incurs zero accountability on their behalf. If no documented commitments are made prior to the test, ***the buyer can do what they want, when they want, with no consequences***.

For example, a buyer provides a new supplier an opportunity to use a small percentage of their store base to test their product. The test product includes both a duplication of existing product under a different brand as well as new product with different options for the consumer at a slightly higher cost. The supplier receives no documented information on what the buyer is trying to accomplish, how the test would be conducted, or for how long. Because the information is so ambiguous, the supplier could be under the impression that they were replacing the existing product in total in the test, when in fact, their product could have been added to the existing program in non-accessible space for the customer. When the supplier asks the buyer about sales expectations, the buyer offers a very minimal amount of information without much value.

In this scenario, it's quite possible the new/prospective supplier perceives the buyer's intention as working to solve existing problems with their current supplier through the threat of a change. If there are unresolved issues the buyer wants resolved, e.g. high returns, which have created tension within the existing relationship, they may introduce a new supplier into the equation to drive leverage. Usually there is no intention of entering a long-term relationship with the new supplier. Over time, a buyer will earn a reputation for this type of activity, which will significantly reduce future opportunities and increase their overall cost of doing business.

By contrast, a merchant will provide clear specifics regarding the current challenges. These could include but are not limited to:

- Low sales
- High returns
- Low margins
- Lack of innovation in a product or segment of their business

A merchant would offer data specifics on what the expectations should be to deem the test a success. The data will be visible to all parties and tracked over a reasonable period. It should include information-tracking that compares a test vs. an agreed-upon base weekly or monthly. Longer periods of time are difficult to justify because they leave little room for adjustments over the life of the test.

There will also be a defined expectation at the end of the test that drives action. Either the supplier has not met expectations and no additional action is needed, or the supplier meets the expectations and there is a defined result on what happens next -- including timing and benefit for both parties. Prior to initiating the test, both parties discuss, agree upon, and document the specifics. Furthermore, if there's an incumbent supplier who could possibly be impacted in a negative way, they are made aware of the test, why the test is taking place, and what the result could be. If a merchant has already given the incumbent supplier an opportunity to solve the need, the test should never come as a surprise to them.

## Sin #9
## Ignoring Verbal or Written Commitments

By far, the most damaging behavior a buyer can exhibit is ignoring verbal or written commitments. It makes a monumental impact on the buyer and the organization, not to mention the cost associated with its accompanying risk. Often, when commitments are broken, it's a direct result of:

- Ambiguous dialogue
- Poor planning
- Poor documentation

- Lack of communication (including delays)

Almost all the behaviors mentioned thus far can lead to this type of conclusion by a supplier -- regardless if it is real or perceived, intentional or unintentional. As noted, a buyer can use the lack of documentation and identifiable commitment to provide flexibility in decision-making without consequence. The end result? An extremely prohibitive cost associated with the risk driven by this behavior. A merchant, on the other hand, documents their commitments with a supplier and drives mutually clear communication to an agreed-upon result. The commitment is defined and rarely ambiguous. If, in fact, the merchant does not deliver on their portion of the commitment (which will happen from time- to- time due to the complexity of the environment they operate in), they will own the consequences and work to a reasonable solution amenable to all parties.

## Sin #10

### Overlook the Risky Behaviors and Their Negative Results

Assuming you identify with one or more of the behaviors I've described, I challenge you to calculate the associated costs. In my experience, it can easily start at a minimum of five percent, upwards to double-digits. If you don't ascribe any of these behaviors as your own, then this perspective isn't for you. You are the consummate merchant. Regrettably, I do not know any merchants who haven't at one time, or another, exhibited one or more of these risky behaviors -- many simultaneously. Due to their own egos and other factors, a buyer doesn't recognize their own faults and has no desire to change, which means they will always pay a higher cost. By contrast, a merchant will instantly recognize the opportunity the harmful behavior has created and correct it. This rewards them with a low-risk reputation, reduced cost associated with overall risk, and access to opportunities other buyers will never experience that could lead to the growth of their business and a reduction in their costs.

4

# TODAY'S MERCHANT

TODAY'S new merchant has a much more difficult role to play than any merchant in the past. Thanks to numerous changes in the way we conduct business, the consequential pressure and stress demands a talent prerequisite that quite frankly, does not yet exist. With the help of the available data, organizations have been quick to recognize opportunities; however, the speed with which they are being created doesn't match the skill set to organize and manage them without creating:

- Confusion
- Complexity
- Lost opportunity
- Risk

In fact, while organizations believe they are gaining cost opportunities and efficiencies through data identification, in many cases, they are in direct conflict with the unidentified cost incurred from trying to manage it. To sum it up, organizations have given free rein to the talent expected to manage this piece of the puzzle with the supplier community -- without guidance or a sustainable structure. This has resulted in the unintended creation of a variety of cost managers, data scientists, and cost-based buyers, all of whom tend to lack the ability to manage a complex relationship - a skill that is needed to mitigate the cost of risk.

So now what?

## 5
## HOW TO GET THERE

ORGANIZATIONS MUST ADOPT VERY specific methodologies and behaviors to drive how they develop and maintain relationships with suppliers.

**Stop driving results primarily based on individual metrics instead of overall improvements.** This mindset divides an organization. The complexity of the business with multiple channels drives multifaceted data sets, each owned by a business group that is responsible for providing value to the organization. In most cases, these groups are compensated by their individual results, which leads to more change. Most companies view the internal competitive environment it creates as a positive, but it often divides the organization into adversarial groups that want to accomplish their own agendas...even at the cost of other pieces of the business they don't own. This usually results in moving costs around rather than solving them.

In terms of a supplier, the merchant must have the support of the organization to be the single business-owner who decides which changes are best for the business -- with responsibility to achieve the maximum overall value -- rather than the lowest cost to consumers. If there are company directives, the merchant should own the timing, planning, and execution with the supplier. The supplier relationship, including execution, cannot be anchored on committee-based decisions. It must be managed by a single owner. That single owner is the merchant who holds an expectation of achieving the highest possible value, not the lowest possible cost.

**Develop, document, and maintain short- and long-term goals with suppliers**. Most key suppliers require agreed upon objectives developed by the merchant and supplier with timelines, tollgates, and defined accountability to derive a benefit for both parties. It must contain a manageable number of value-driven objectives for both the supplier and the organization. It should also include:

- A joint quarterly review showing the project and specific tollgates on a predetermined and collaborative timeline.
- The owner of each tollgate in terms of execution.
- Expected results.

To ensure all activity drives value, every project needs a defined and trackable outcome. Time and action strategies offer a productive method of planning joint projects, tracking completion, achieving results, managing workload, and maintaining stability in the relationship. It should have a one- to- five-year forward-looking view that is updated on a consistent basis, ideally quarterly. If a particular action or project is not on the joint time and action plan, then it hasn't been mutually agreed to and neither the merchant nor the supplier should spend resources on it.

. . .

**Understand cost vs. value and what is most important to the consumer**. Cost buyers manage every individual item to its lowest available cost, which puts pressure on every item in a supplier's portfolio. Results of this type of negotiation many times results in reduced quality in the product as the supplier tries to reach an unreasonable cost expectation by the buyer. This type of action also drives a very low profitability opportunity for suppliers and leads to a diminished relationship. Good merchants manage entire programs to their highest consumer-recognized value. The market has shown repeatedly consumers are willing to pay a value proposition for those items that solve their issues -- whether time, work, or health-related. True, some items with the lowest prices in the market represent the total value proposition; for example, milk, eggs, and bread, which we recognize as staples. However, even these categories offer opening, mid, high, and premium-priced products with less sensitivity to retail. These types of products exist in all categories.

There are items up the continuum with premium features that -- due to the lower level of price sensitivity -- can drive a higher level of overall profitability for both the supplier and the merchant. A merchant will leverage the premium items against the more price-sensitive products to promote value while increasing demand in the market and maximizing profit. Suppliers use a similar strategy that is acknowledged by merchants and both sides of the equation work together to present the best overall value to the market. Margin expectations must be managed at the program level, not at the item level. In addition, merchants drive their programs based on what the market will bear, not to a gross margin. Gross-margin growth should be a derivative of joint planning in reducing and managing costs and adding innovation with new product -- not joint planning in what to charge to get to a specific margin.

When a supplier asks for the margin requirements, or the buyer asks to make a specific margin instead of promoting a higher value, these specific conversations create substantial risk.

**Create supplier relationships with value at all levels of the organization but maintain one point of control.** So long as a merchant is using documented short- and long-term time and action plans, maintaining control of the relationship becomes a core competency. When someone in the organization other than the merchant (such as an executive from operations, supply chain, marketing, etc.), interacts with a supplier, it's a meaningful way to organize conversation when an existing, documented plan is shared with all parties. Others in the organization who have feedback on changes they see that may be needed in the relationship will funnel opportunities exclusively through the merchant and not directly to the supplier. The result will help to maintain a single point of contact and avoid disruption or confusion in the relationship. The more consistent the interaction and understanding of initiatives between the supplier and the organization at every level, the lower the risk is in the relationship between the two.

**Institute a sustainable merchant development program driving consistency in behaviors.** Due to the speed in which the market changes and its accompanying complexity, an ever-increasing number of associates are needed to manage the business -- which also creates unavoidable turnover. If a company has no organized method of developing, sustaining, and improving the behaviors discussed, risk will always be a significant issue to manage along with the associated rising costs. Here are some valuable practices that can minimize risk:

- Institute working classroom instruction giving specific examples and discussing desired vs. undesirable behaviors for merchants.
- Assign mentors to incoming merchants so they can observe the desired behaviors in real-time situations.
- Re-evaluate those in merchant positions today to make sure skill sets meet the desired behavioral results and make any necessary changes.
- Do not place associates in merchant positions who can't exhibit the skill set to manage a complex business and the associated relationships.
- Insist the organization adopt a merchant-based management platform in which all levels recognize, support, and understand the complexity of the relationships being managed.
- Have a documented and clearly understood succession plan supporting the overall needs to develop merchants on an ongoing and sustainable basis.

**Develop merchants who have the confidence to make timely decisions and own the results, both positive and negative.** It will take a significant cultural effort to create an environment where merchants are not creating risk out of fear of failure. Although producing results is critical in the current competitive environment, it can come at the expense of developing an atmosphere of confusion and fear, due to the leadership behaviors. To instill confidence and build merchants, the management team must recognize results and effort, both mutually and exclusively of one another. When a merchant experiences a negative result or a competitive pressure they hadn't planned for, it creates a vital learning opportunity; their leadership should teach and train -- not punish and ridicule. Yes, it is imperative to hold merchants accountable for achieving set goals, but this accountability must accompany positive reinforcement to produce greater confidence and ultimately better performance.

**Create an observed and *validated* outlet for suppliers to ask for change.** Most organizations have no outlet for suppliers to ask for help in solving for specific situations that occur between suppliers and merchants. In many cases, the supplier feels stuck or pinned down with a unique issue or problem with a buyer where resolution has stalled and is driving negativity in the relationship. To resolve the situation, suppliers tend to hire consultants with experience in the industry to provide guidance and a supplemental strategy for navigating a poorly constructed relationship between a supplier and a buyer. Many times, the consultation is based purely on the consultant's ability to communicate with others in the organization they have existing relationships with. If a supplier could access the same advice without having to hire an outside consultant, imagine the opportunities it would create for positive change?

While multiple organizations believe they already provide such an outlet due to the structure and accessibility of their leadership, its rarely used. A buyer's lack of confidence will drive them to caution a supplier against contacting anyone in management, out of fear of retribution or damage to their reputation. Uncovering that negative behavior and correcting it through example is one of the most difficult challenges an organization can face: if a buyer doesn't want anyone else in the organization talking to one of their suppliers at the supplier's request, it's a red flag that must be addressed. Most often, it leads to the discovery of problems with supplier relationships, most often created by poor management on the buyer's part, and in many instances, reveals several short-sighted decisions. The leadership must exhibit behaviors that support both the merchant and supplier in resolving conflict: there is no need for either one to feel diminished by the outcome. Both must agree to the plan of action. In such a scenario, leadership becomes the teacher, trainer, and mediator, thus reducing risk through more positive behaviors. It eventually drives a higher level of supplier and merchant confidence that there are outlets for fair resolution between the two when needed, without retribution. In all considerations, both sides of the equation must be represented and involved.

**Create a consistent opening discussion within the organization between a supplier and a merchant.** One of the most crucial periods in any new relationship is the initial dialogue. It's important for the merchant to create trust and clarity in the very first interaction, regardless of where the relationship goes from there. This interaction also lends itself to creating a positive or negative reputation for an organization, depending on the consistency of these conversations. For example, in the opening discussion, a merchant must exhibit true interest in the supplier, the product or service they provide, what they want to accomplish, and their overall goals in the market. If a merchant understands how they can contribute to reaching a supplier's specific goals while formulating whether a supplier can benefit their own organization, it drives a more positive conversation with an opportunity to also drive positive results. Look at it from the perspective of "what can you do for the supplier," before you get into "what the supplier can do for you."

This practice of looking out for both the supplier's and the organization's interests will immediately reduce the real or perceived amount of risk the supplier may feel they are entering. The initial conversation consists of asking questions, listening, and then communicating the supplier's potential opportunities with clarity. When the supplier leaves the first meeting, they should walk away with a clear and concise set of follow-up actions or a good understanding of why there is no current opportunity. A merchant always obtains a detailed picture of who the supplier is, what position they hold in the market, and the opportunities they may create now or in the future for the organization. Every supplier who isn't a supplier of yours is most likely a supplier for one of your competitors; regardless of the direction the relationship takes, there are always learning opportunities.

**Create a merchant behavior that recognizes and mitigates the 3 primary "games" suppliers tend to play when negotiating or managing the relationship.** Each can be as detrimental as the poor behavior by some buyers. To keep their costs at a comfortable level, (remember, they are adding cost to mitigate the risk they are experiencing on top of their real/identified costs), suppliers will engage in several poor practices that the merchant must recognize and manage:

. . .

**1.) A supplier will expect and make requests to cover the costs associated with changing market conditions.**

For example, the rising cost of healthcare is a dynamic the total market deals with on both sides of the equation. For the supplier, the easiest way to resolve the issue is to pass along the expense to the merchant, pointing to the changing market conditions as the driver. What a supplier *should* be doing is working within its own structure to maintain their current cost by creating efficiencies within their own operations...not passing it along.

In such cases, a merchant should recognize and acknowledge the market dynamics that drive new costs, then partner with the supplier to identify efficiencies both can enact to mitigate the changing market. If a supplier can't demonstrate this specific activity on an ongoing basis regarding creating efficiencies (especially when the volume is growing), the relationship isn't built on the right expectations and principals, and the merchant should refuse to engage in cost increases. The merchant has every right to ask for and understand the factors behind the way in which their specific cost is structured from a supplier.

Asking for detail and understanding of what comprises cost can be an essential tool in the relationship if the supplier is willing to share the information. As mentioned earlier, these details include:

**Raw Materials + Manufacturing + G&A + Supply**

**Chain + Distribution + Marketing + Gross Margin + Risk = Cost**

With knowledge of where the costs originate and recognition of existing opportunities to create efficiency, both parties can manage costs in the relationship. However, many suppliers will not share this information, due to having imbedded margin into many of the cost contributors...which should be a warning sign in the relationship. Either the supplier engages in subpar practices or doesn't trust the merchant, or the merchant hasn't exhibited a willingness to be fair and understand the detail in the relationship so both can work toward mutual benefits. The result is detrimental to mitigating cost driven by risk.

Ask for the cost detail within any program or item you are buying. A supplier who will not share this information will drive a different and more difficult relationship with significantly lower opportunities to create benefits. Remember, the information a supplier shares with you must be managed for the mutual benefit of both in the relationship to reduce the cost associated with risk. In addition, there are times the market does require passing along costs from the supplier to the merchant and ultimately from the merchant to the consumer to keep the relationship balanced. A good merchant recognizes those specific circumstances and acts accordingly. A good example is activity around international tariffs that may be imposed between countries that are obviously unavoidable for all involved.

**2) A supplier will engage in the same ambiguous**

**activity a buyer might exhibit when communicating or agreeing on a program.**

For example, negotiating and agreeing on several parameters around the relationship with respect to a rebate, marketing, or other backdoor funding without any documentation. If the supplier changes sales associates or executive teams, suddenly the conversations are no longer verifiable and agreements go by the wayside, thus creating a substantial amount of animosity in the relationship. This can be a very common occurrence in relationships built on a handshake vs. documented details between both parties, and the cost associated with this type of risk can be substantial for the merchant. Always make it a practice to require documentation for conversations that involve any agreement between a merchant and the supplier -- especially agreements that are not included in the formal buy/sell contract between the two companies. It can be as simple as an email between both parties, which in most cases is as binding as a contract extension unless it's specifically called out in the email not to be. Even if non-binding, it's still has substantial value in the ongoing management of the relationship to maintain good documentation. In the end, this practice will result in the elimination of the "who said what" activity.

### 3) The person representing the supplier to the merchant isn't the negotiator.

This is a common tactic in which suppliers intentionally send in representatives to meet with a merchant who are required to ask permission "from their boss" for any decision regarding the program. It gives the supplier the advantage of an "out" in a negotiation and the time to weigh the circumstances and plan accordingly while they keep the merchant "outside of the discussion." To avoid this outcome, a merchant should always negotiate with the supplier representative who has the authority to make decisions. It helps to develop a "face-to-face" relationship that can be built on trust and integrity...instead of creating a scenario where the merchant has the disadvantage of always negotiating with a third party they have not met. This circumstance with a supplier should not be supported in the relationship.

# EPILOGUE

***This isn't a business issue that data will ever solve; it's one-hundred percent behavioral dependent.***

RECENTLY, actual suppliers who operate in the retail market made several key comments about their relationships with buyers. Their feedback reinforces the need for buyers to examine and change their behaviors to reduce the risks associated with them. I've intentionally removed suppliers' names, specific buyers, locations, types of products, and any other information that could lead to the identification of the suppliers and their retailers to maintain confidentiality. However, to uphold the integrity and quality of the message, the comments themselves are accurate. All the suppliers who provided input preferred to be anonymous in the publication to avoid any possible retribution, which is a negative perception caused by bad behaviors. Although this represents a small segment of the supplier population in numbers, these are extremely large suppliers who own a significant share in the market. Their comments remain consistent with what I regularly hear when discussing the challenges of the supplier/buyer relationships, regardless of size.

**Supplier #1:**

- Due to paralysis by analysis, buyers are either afraid or unable to make decisions. Their fear is rooted in the intense pressure their companies put on them to hit their performance matrix. If they fail, they lose their job.
- Failure to respond to emails or calls. As the new associates take on buyer/merchant positions, this is happening more frequently.
- Since many merchants lack the proper experience, there is a very long learning curve.
- High turnover in merchant positions creates a lack of continuity in executing longer term strategies to grow a program as a partner.
- Buyers are either too busy or overwhelmed with responsibilities.

**Supplier #2:**

- Lack of communication.
- Margin focus that impacts/holds back revenue.
- Avoiding candid conversations.
- Failure to look beyond the near term.
- Lack of collaboration.

## Supplier #3: Margins

- Although margins are important to both the merchant and the manufacturer, oftentimes the merchant only thinks about their own profit. It causes the manufacturer to exhibit different behaviors such as varying product components that make the product cheaper in the eyes of the consumer. It's common to be asked by a consumer if they should buy from big box retail or a trade showroom because they hear that there are differences in the quality of products sold at retail.
- The manufacturer believes that the margin discussion is always one-sided...in favor of the merchants.
- We could both win long term if the payback on a product launch was longer than 6-12 months. Merchants are quick to determine the success or failure of a product within this timeframe, yet all for all other channels in which we do business, the payback is 12-24 months.
- Merchants are not willing to pay for innovation and technology in product; however, they are the first ones to ask for it.

## Short-Term Thinking by the Merchant

- The merchants are looking for immediate payback on a new product launch or program. If it doesn't work in 6 months, they are onto something else.

- As most big box retailers are publicly traded companies, their thinking is quarter to quarter.
- If the merchants could act and think as small, nimble, flexible businesses, I believe the results would be much different.

### Little Time Spent on Strategizing with the Manufacturer

- There must be more time devoted to working on mutual strategies and developing plans to drive growth.
- The merchant doesn't have the time, take the time, or possess the skills to think long term about "what could be" with their strategic partners. It's a huge problem with many of today's merchants.

### Too Much Time Spent by the Merchant on Non-revenue Issues

- Merchants today have an incredibly full plate and many of the tasks they deal with are not productive in terms of driving new business.
- If the merchant could spend less time dealing with fines, returns, consumer issues, fill rates, forecasting, plan-o-grams, supply chain negotiations etc., together we could drive more business.

- I have heard that merchants can spend as much as 40% of their time on these types of issues.

**The Merchant Doesn't Always Trust the Manufacturer's Research**

- The manufacturer does extensive research on styles, designs, innovation etc.
- When we bring this information to the merchant, they question our research methods, results and recommendations.
- The merchant must demonstrate more trust that we have done our homework and are bringing the merchant the best product at the best price

Everything you read above in terms of what suppliers think about buyers/merchants is addressed in this perspective, and change is possible. The result will be a reduced risk that produces positive results, which will be passed along to the consumer in the form of increased value -- whether it be in cost or in features and quality.

# WRITTEN EXERCISES

It's important to put in a few minutes of additional work to take advantage of the learnings this book provides. Thinking about each of the negative behaviors will help you self-identify how you react to each situation. Personalizing the "10 Sins of a Buyer" will help to maximize your own positive change, creating new opportunities for reduced cost and increased value in your business.

Take each "deadly sin" for a buyer and answer the following regarding your behaviors:

- Do I recognize this detrimental behavior in my day-to-day activity and if so, what is the specific behavior I exhibit?
- What behavior should I be exhibiting to avoid making this mistake?

**Example Sin:** "I don't take calls or respond to the communication from a supplier who is new to the organization or the industry."

**Behavior I currently exhibit** I pass along calls from suppliers I don't do business with to my assistant to manage without any follow up by me.

**Behavior I will exhibit in the future:** I will take the initial call from a supplier I am not currently doing business with at the time it comes in. If I am not able to take the call, I will pass it along to my assistant and instruct them to get the pertinent information for me to call them back within 72 hours.

**Complete the following responses based on your own personal behaviors:**

**1) "Not taking a call or responding to the communication from a supplier who is new to the organization or the industry."**

Behavior I currently exhibit:

_______________________________________________

_______________________________________________

_______________________________________________

_______________________________________________

Behavior I will exhibit in the future:

_______________________________________________

_______________________________________________

_______________________________________________

_______________________________________________

**2) "Ignoring the calls or creating a significant delay in responding to the communication from an existing supplier."**

Behavior I currently exhibit:

_______________________________________________

_______________________________________________

_______________________________________________

_______________________________________________

Behavior I will exhibit in the future:

_______________________________________________

_______________________________________________

_______________________________________________

_______________________________________________

**3) "Ignoring the short- and long-term goals important to a supplier."**

Behavior I currently exhibit:

---------------------------------------------------

---------------------------------------------------

---------------------------------------------------

---------------------------------------------------

Behavior I will exhibit in the future:

---------------------------------------------------

---------------------------------------------------

---------------------------------------------------

---------------------------------------------------

---------------------------------------------------

**4) "Allowing the organization to run the relationship between the supplier and the buyer."**

Behavior I currently exhibit:

---------------------------------------------------

---------------------------------------------------

---------------------------------------------------

---------------------------------------------------

Behavior I will exhibit in the future:

---------------------------------------------------

---------------------------------------------------

---------------------------------------------------

---------------------------------------------------

---------------------------------------------------

**5) "Poor planning driving unreasonable expectations."**

Behavior I currently exhibit:

______________________________________________

______________________________________________

______________________________________________

______________________________________________

Behavior I will exhibit in the future:

______________________________________________

______________________________________________

______________________________________________

______________________________________________

______________________________________________

**6) "Surprising a supplier with the loss of business."**

Behavior I currently exhibit:

______________________________________________

______________________________________________

______________________________________________

______________________________________________

Behavior I will exhibit in the future:

______________________________________________

______________________________________________

______________________________________________

______________________________________________

______________________________________________

**7) "Being friends instead of business partners."**

Behavior I currently exhibit:

________________________________________________

________________________________________________

________________________________________________

________________________________________________

________________________________________________

Behavior I will exhibit in the future:

________________________________________________

________________________________________________

________________________________________________

________________________________________________

________________________________________________

**8) "Ambiguity in the relationship created by the buyer."**

Behavior I currently exhibit:

________________________________________________

________________________________________________

________________________________________________

________________________________________________

Behavior I will exhibit in the future:

________________________________________________

________________________________________________

________________________________________________

________________________________________________

________________________________________________

**9) "Ignoring commitments, verbal or written."**

Behavior I currently exhibit:

_______________________________________________

_______________________________________________

_______________________________________________

_______________________________________________

Behavior I will exhibit in the future:

_______________________________________________

_______________________________________________

_______________________________________________

_______________________________________________

_______________________________________________

**10) "Ignore the risky behaviors without recognizing the negative results they create."**

Behavior I currently exhibit:

_______________________________________________

_______________________________________________

_______________________________________________

_______________________________________________

Behavior I will exhibit in the future:

_______________________________________________

_______________________________________________

_______________________________________________

_______________________________________________

_______________________________________________

## ABOUT THE AUTHOR

* * *

Mike Hogenmiller is a 40-plus year veteran of the retail home improvement industry. His experience includes both operations and merchandising at the executive level where he was directly responsible for businesses with annual revenues of more than six-billion dollars. Mike's background encompasses wholesale and retail associated with brick-and-mortar, along with the e-Commerce channels. During his career, his individual merchant responsibilities had an annualized volume ranging from as little as $100,000 to as much as $400,000,000 in revenues with a single supplier giving him experience in managing a wide range of complex businesses. Mike also served as a mentor to several leaders both inside and outside of the industry through organizations such as American Corporate Partners. Certified as a Green Belt in Six Sigma, he has taught and trained others in proprietary programs developed by several of the companies he served. Although he retired from the industry in 2016, Mike continues to work as an industry consultant for multiple domestic and international organizations. He and his wife Nancy now married for more than 42 years, are very much enjoying retirement by spending time with their daughter Jillian and son and daughter in-law Michael and Hunter. All currently reside in Atlanta Georgia. You can reach him via email at HogenmillerConsulting@gmail.com or private messaging on LinkedIn.com.

www.ingramcontent.com/pod-product-compliance
Lightning Source LLC
LaVergne TN
LVHW050946080826
845145LV00004B/1426

* 9 7 8 0 5 7 8 5 4 3 9 7 0 *